YOUR KNOWLEDGE HAS

Ivaldir Honório de Farias Júnior, Alinne Corrêa dos Santos, Marcelo Mendonça Teixeira, Tiago Alessandro Espínola Ferreira

Factors and Effects of Communication in Distributed Software Development

GRIN Verlag

Bibliografische Information der Deutschen Nationalbibliothek:

Die Deutsche Bibliothek verzeichnet diese Publikation in der Deutschen National-
bibliografie; detaillierte bibliografische Daten sind im Internet über http://dnb.d-
nb.de/ abrufbar.

Imprint:

Copyright © 2014 GRIN Verlag GmbH
Druck und Bindung: Books on Demand GmbH, Norderstedt Germany
ISBN: 978-3-656-57182-7

This book at GRIN:

http://www.grin.com/en/e-book/266728/factors-and-effects-of-communication-in-
distributed-software-development

GRIN - Your knowledge has value

Der GRIN Verlag publiziert seit 1998 wissenschaftliche Arbeiten von Studenten, Hochschullehrern und anderen Akademikern als eBook und gedrucktes Buch. Die Verlagswebsite www.grin.com ist die ideale Plattform zur Veröffentlichung von Hausarbeiten, Abschlussarbeiten, wissenschaftlichen Aufsätzen, Dissertationen und Fachbüchern.

Visit us on the internet:

http://www.grin.com/

http://www.facebook.com/grincom

http://www.twitter.com/grin_com

Factors and Effects of Communication in Distributed Software Development

Ivaldir Honório de Farias Junior

Alinne Corrêa dos Santos

Marcelo Mendonça Teixeira

Tiago Alessandro Espínola Ferreira

January 2014

"I'm a great believer that any tool that enhances communication
has profound effects in terms of how people can learn from each
other, and how they can achieve the kind of freedoms that they're
interested in"

Bill Gates

INDEX

Introduction

Cybercommunication   1

Research Method   2

The Results So Far   3

Analysis of Results   4

Proposal of Good Practices   5

Final Considerations   6

Tertiary Study Limitations   7

Acknowledgments   8

References   9

Introduction

The global interaction based on the sharing of information and knowledge, and advances in communication technologies, have changed the concept of economy and society - consumers become producers, and producers become consumers of content, goods and services in a new global economic model, without restrictions or barriers, induced by a process of massive collaboration, say Tapscott and Williams in Teixeira (2012). In its turn, the "Information Society" has become a natural stage in the evolutionary and social development of people, in a world increasingly interconnected by new technologies. Manuel Castells adds to that, asserting that the web allowed interest groups and network projects to overcome time-costs problems associated to the chaotic pre-www information, as, in this basis, groups, individuals and organizations could interact significantly with what has become, literally, a wide world web of interactive and individualized communication. Thence, a new social conscience is created, which will be used by an net society, at local and global levels, crossing both communication contexts, constituting a collaborative e interactive global network. In other sense, the geographical boundaries are diluted, the world today is interconnected by the simultaneity of the new information and communication technologies.

In other sense, the literature and industrial practice reveal that the Distributed Software Development (DSD) is becoming a reality in most large organizations, in search of improvements in quality, productivity and cost reduction. However, although several (primary and secondary) studies have produced results for the communication process in DSD design, there is still a lack of a Systematic Tertiary Study to provide subsidies for further research and improvement on industrial practice. Our book aims at a conceptual approach concerning DSD design and consolidates knowledge about the communication process in DSD projects, especially the factors that influence the communication, the effects of communication in DSD projects and the relationship between factors and effects.

Erran Carmel (1999) in "Global Software Teams – Collaborating Across Borders and Time-Zones", covers the definition of global and virtual development teams and the most essential aspects to be considered when creating a DSD workgroup. The author suggests the existence of five categories that may lead a distributed team in the decline or failure of the project. They are: inefficient communication, lack of coordination, geographic dispersion, loss of workgroup spirit and cultural differences, called centrifugal force. In this sense, we will explore the communication in DSD in our book based on systematic Literature Review.

The global software development generated a new era in software development by eliminating boundary of development team in recent decade. However, distributed software development has its own challenges and implementation of agile software development in it further brings the challenges due to their contradictory practices, concludes Bhalerao and Ingle (2009).

1. Cybercommunication

The term "Cybernetics" stems from the Greek "kubernetes" (steersman, that who steers, who controls, who governs), which was designed by the philosopher Plato[1]. Historically, the conceptual prelude acknowledged by the international scientific community is credited to Norbert Wiener in his "Cybernetics: Or Control and Communication in the Animal and Machine", published in 1948. However, Wiener (1984) recognizes that the word had already been used by the French physicist André-Marie Ampère (Cybernétique, in 1834), in a Science Political context. Laclau and Luhmann (2006, p.52) are categorical in asserting that Wiener's connotation was different from Ampère's one, because he defines cybernetics as "the scientific study of control and communication in the animal and the machine". Chiavenato (2004) states that as well as an applied science, it was limited to the creation of machines of self-regulating behaviour with similar aspects to human or animal behaviour (such as a robot, a computer - which was called "electronic brain" - , and a radar, based on bats behaviour; a plane autopilot, etc). Subsequently, according to the same researcher, cybernetics applications were extended to other scientific areas, such as Engineering, Biology, Medicine, Psychology, Mathematics, Sociology and Computer Science.

At this time, Cyber Era sprang up, thus becoming the parent of cyberspace, cyberschool, cyberdemocracy, cyberpunk, cyberpolitics, cyberlaw, cybercommunication, cybersociety…, which are, in Norman Lee Johnson's perception, prodigal elements of symbiotic intelligence, and which are also so much discussed in the literary works of Douglas Hofstadter, Peter Russell, Jean Baudrillard, Gottfried Mayer-Kress, Howard Bloom, Steven Johnson, Pierre Lévy, as Collective Intelligence (synonym for cyberculture). Nevertheless, robots, computers and their electronic components preceded modern cybernetics, and they were responsible for the evolution from mass society (industrialized and mediatised) to the network society (communitarian and globalized).

---

[1]Etymologically, the term dates back to VI century B.C., when, according to the Greek mythology, Theseus travelled to Crete on a boat steered by two steersmen (Chiavenato, 2004). To glorify this successful trip, Theseus organized a party to the "cybernetics", the pilots of the sea. Later, Plato (427-347 B.C.) used the word "Kybernytiky" in his dialogues "Alcibiades" and "Gorgias", meaning "the art of piloting a ship", in "Clitophon", meaning "the art of leading men" and in "The Republic", meaning "the art of ruling, in general" (ibidem). Following Plato's rhetoric, Ampère gives to this ancient word a socio-political meaning (control, government, leading). For decades, these meanings kept a considerable influence in different areas of knowledge, such as mathematics, physics, electronics, medicine, psychology, chemistry, mechanics and computer science (especially, if related to artificial intelligence).

In the 60's and 70's, computing was developed in research universities and labs, which were a privilege for a few ones. Thus, in these research centres, some selective visionary and enthusiast programmers groups were established, such as Robert Noyce, Steve Jobs, Steve Wozniack and Bill Gates, the so called Silicon Valley residents[2]. In 1960, Theodor Holm Nelson brings about the computing "eureka moment"[3] through the Project Xanadu (theoretical basis to the World Wide Web and network communication). Inspired by Memex[4], a work by scientist Vannevar Bush, in 1963 Ted established the terms "hypertext" and "hypermedia", which were published in 1965 in "Complex information processing: A file structure for the complex, the changing and the indeterminate". In the hypertext, he clearly paraphrases Memex ground basis in order to make up for human memory limitations through informational trails interrelated by association in words, terms, acronyms and ideas in a non-linear way. In its turn, hypermedia, as an extension of the hypertext concept, is a combination of multiple media elements (text, audio, video and image) sustained by a computational structure and mediated by synchronous and asynchronous digital communication systems. In the following years, the terms "link" and "hyperlink" emerged to refer to an electronic hypertext document or to a specific element within another different document.

In 1970, the counterculture movements interpreted hyperlink principles as a way of unite people through communication by preaching non-violence (caused by Vietnam War). At the same time, the international Oil Crisis and the Watergate scandal[5] motivated media technological development and, once again, the global communication for the exchange of information and news between geographically dispersed countries. Coincidentally, Barbosa and Canesso (2004) point out that at this time a civic motion arises aiming at the creation of network communities in North America (Teixeira, 2012).

---

[2]The Valley is situated in California (USA), which is home to many of the world's largest technology corporations and manufacturers, since the 50's.
[3]Famous term used to refer to an important finding or an accomplishment of great relevance. The credits for the origin of the word are attributed to the Greek philosopher Archimedes.
[4]In 1945, Bush published in The Atlantic Monthly magazine the paper "As We May Think", in which he wrote about a machine (Memex - Memory Extension) that would have the task of helping human memory to store knowledge. He suggested a structure to organize contents in a non-hierarchical way and of non-linear access based on a mechanic device for individual use, to save texts, registers, communications and books, in order to make the search for information easier and more flexible (Gosciola, 2003).
[5]A political scandal that occurred in the United States in the 70's and which led to President Richard Nixon's resignation.

From 1972 to 1974, some movements sprang up in Berkeley and San Francisco (California), such as "Computers for the People" and "Community Memory"[6], respectively. The latter was intended to create a network of shared information, similar to an electronic bulletin board without a central control, where people could enter information (Wiki prototype)[7]or read it in the most convenient way to each of them (Torres, 2011). To do so, they used a terminals network spread throughout the Pacific States[8], i.e. Alaska, California, Hawaii, Oregon and Washington. This project represented the development of alternative media that could be used by the community to produce information related to their common needs and interests, i.e. an attempt to use computer communication effectiveness to serve the community (ibidem). In addition, as pointed out by Barbosa and Canesso (2004), it became a model for network communities around the world, usually established to make easier the free exchange of information, such as libraries and philanthropic entities, which exchanged information through e-mails, forum debates and texts writing (collective authorship). Cyberculture flourishes in this scenario, being its genesis influenced by the first network communication movements.

1.2 Simulacres et Simulation in Information Society

In the late 80's and early 90's, a new sociocultural movement, originated by young professionals in big American cities and universities, reached a global dimension, and with no agency to limit that process, the different computer networks developed in the 70's joined together, while the number of people and computers connected to the network grew very fast (Vanassi, 2007). Thirty years of continuous growth of society and collective intelligence virtualization led to the Millennial Generation (or Generation Y), going from the operating system ENQUIRE development, by Timothy John Berners-Lee, and following Ted Nelson's Xanadu and Hypertetx principles to culminate in the World Wide Web, in 1989. Progressively, the Web evolved from a static guideline (1.0) to a collaborative one (2.0), and after that to a guideline of contents portability, information connectivity and programming languages integration (3.0). Experts already talk about an artificial intelligence Web (4.0), as foreseen by

---

[6]It was brought into existence, under Project One, by Efrem Lipkin, Szpakowski Mark and Lee Felsenstein, in San Francisco in 1973.
[7]It allows Internet users to create and edit text on a specific Web page using any Web browser.
[8]North American States which are bounded by the Pacific Ocean on the West.

Anandarajan and Anandarajan (2010). At the same time, numerous interactive resources are developed for the Internet and media digitalization.

But such a phenomenon, as Jean Baudrillard writes in his "Simulacres et Simulation", does not necessarily represent the techno-cultural-communicative excellence. According to this work, reality does not exist anymore, and we are now living its representation, widespread by the media and mass media in post-modern society (Revista Superinteressante, 2005). Being ironic, but well-reasoned, Baudrillard stands for the theory that we live in a time in which symbols are more important than reality itself. This phenomenon leads to the so called "simulacra" – bad reality simulations that, contradictorily, are more attractive to the audience than the imitated object itself (ibidem), what, in the words of Haesbaert (2004), causes feelings of dispossession and multiterritoriality. Baudrillard's philosophical critique particularly falls upon the consumer society and the media overvaluation, and he also rejects the Global Village concept, which he thinks is a distant and utopian reality.

Paralelly, Mark Bauerlein goes further in his "The dumbest generation: How the digital age stupefies young Americans and jeopardizes our future", by accusing the digital era of stupefying and idiotizing American young people through anomy, isolation, addiction and cognitive overload. Other authors, like Oliveira (2011), do not agree completely with Baudrillard or Bauerlein, arguing that the digital generation has its pros and cons, as well as past generations and the current generation Z (the connectivity generation). Relations between humans, work and intelligence itself depend on the constant metamorphosis of information devices of all kinds: writing, reading, watching, hearing, creating, learning are captured by a more advanced informatics, and it is no longer possible to conceive scientific research without a complex tool, that distributes old divisions between experience and theory (Lévy, 2010).

In fact, the need of new sociability behaviours promoted new ways of technological development, changing, shifting and creating unusual relations between Man and information and communication technologies (Lemos, 2003). This was exactly what happened at the turn of the 20th century to 21st century when many revolutionary network communication electronic devices were developed. As a consequence of globalization and technological growth, the subsequent multiculturalism established a new social structure, consisting of different kinds of people and corporations, guided by interactions, collaborations and knowledge exchange in the newly adult virtual universe.

On this matter, Paul Virilio calls attention to the temporal dispersion and the loss of sense of reality in cyberspace, some kind of an atopy to the digital natives, deeply absorbed by a great amount of endless information. On the other hand, Howe (2009, p.10) writes that, raised on the basis of social media and always connected to the Internet, digital natives are simultaneously engaged in numerous projects; they easily and spontaneously work together with people they have never seen in their lives and, above all, they create media with the same enthusiasm that previous generations consumed them: "It is a crowdsourcing community, a crowd perfectly adapted to the future in which online communities will overcome the conventional corporations". New technologies also help to "connect" people from different cultures outside the virtual space, what was unthinkable fifty years ago. In this giant relationships web, we mutually absorb each other's beliefs, customs, values, laws and habits, cultural legacies perpetuated by a physical-virtual dynamics in constant metamorphosis (Teixeira, 2013).

Apart from the criticism, with no ideological idyll, we conclude that new lifestyles are permeated by a global culture that enhances new sociability ways in the contemporary world through digital technologies ("sine qua non" principle of the so called "Cyberculture"). In other words, it is a cultural virtualization of human reality as a result of the migration from physical to virtual space (mediated by the ICTs), ruled by codes, signs and particular social relationships. Forwards, arise instant ways of communication, interaction and possible quick access to information, in which we are no longer mere senders, but also producers, reproducers, co-workers and providers. New technologies also help to "connect" people from different cultures outside the virtual space, what was unthinkable fifty years ago. In this giant relationships web, we mutually absorb each other's beliefs, customs, values, laws and habits, cultural legacies perpetuated by a physical-virtual dynamics in constant metamorphosis (ibidem).

To Sailwal (2009), contemporaneously, in global market, software companies are forced to compete with each other and must sustain their competitiveness. Software companies outsource or offshore their work leading to the formation of distributed teams to cut down development costs, availability of skilled labor force, reduce time-to-market of their products, risk sharing, etc. "Despite the fact that distributed software development offers many benefits to software companies, the developers do come across several challenges like culture difference, loss of communication richness, geographical dispersion, coordination breakdown, loss of teamness and time zone differences. Information and communication technologies can minimize these problems but managing the knowledge that exists between the team members, processes, culture, and working environment of the software company is also important", consider the author (p.2).

1.3 Distributed Software Development: Strategies to Business

In recent years, we noticed a movement towards globalization. In particular, the Information Technology (IT) sector has become an important and stimulating sector for organizations, where it is possible to simplify production processes using some solutions in this sector, which consequently increase productivity in organizations. Therefore, this sector has just become a competitive differential among companies, in order to minimize costs and use geographically dispersed resources. This quest for increasing competitiveness has driven organizations to the investment in Distributed Software Development (DSD) (Herbsleb & Moitra, 2001) environments, where great efforts have been made towards research in this context (Prikladnicki, Damian & Audy, 2008).

DSD has been stimulated worldwide and an increasingly significant number of organizations have distributed their processes around the world (Herbsleb, 2007; Carmel, 2005) due to the particularities that differentiate it from traditional development. According to Betz and Makio (2007), about 40% of the distributed projects fail because of their complexity and greater challenges, which make project management more difficult, thus being necessary to use methods, processes and tools which are more suitable for the software engineering distributed context (Binder, 2007; Komi—Sirvio & Tihnen, 2005; Pichler, 2007).

DSD is characterized by physical distance and/or different time-zone among those involved (client, user and team) in the process of software development (Audy & Prikladnicki, 2007). This physical and temporal separation entails some advantages, but it also brings some challenges related to communication, coordination and cooperation in carrying out tasks such as: distance levels between the members, cultural and time-zone differences, lack of standardization processes, tools and infrastructure incompatibility. Among these challenges is worth noting the communication, which is present throughout the life cycle of a software project and permeates all aspects of a project manager's work. Its importance is expressed on the estimate that up to 90% of the time spent in the effort of project management in general is somehow devoted to communications (Mulcahy, 2005; PMI, 2008).

With geographically distributed teams, face-to-face communication turns out to be less frequent and has therefore less impact on projects. Temporal dispersion, especially because of time-zone difference, affects activities such as elicitation, requirement negotiation and changes in scope. Additionally, DSD is also influenced by the cultural differences of the people involved in it, since the project is based on the good relationships established among them.

In this context, understanding the aspects addressed by this communication process in distributed environments becomes an important role for the success of these projects. In his study, Silva (2007) reports that the lack of communication has a great impact on the success/failure of a particular project.

However, although several studies (Silva et al., 2007; Prikladnicki, 2003; Trindade; Meira, Lemos, 2008; Farias Júnior, 2008; Da Silva, Prikladnicki, Franca, Monteiro, Costa & Rocha, 2010) have produced important results in understanding communication process in distributed environments, gaps regarding the consolidation of literature still exist. Therefore this study grounds rely on a better understanding of the influence of communication process, as well as, the possible effects of this influence in DSD projects. At the same time, it aims at consolidating this understanding so that it can be used by researchers and professionals.

In this context, the purpose of this research is to investigate and consolidate knowledge about the communication process in DSD projects, especially the factors that influence the communication, the effects of communication in DSD projects and the relationship between factors and effects. This research is guided by three main research questions:

(Q1) Which factors influence the communication process in Distributed Software Development Projects?

(Q2) Which are the effects identified in the communication process in Distributed Software Development Projects?

(Q3) Which factors identified in Q1 are related to the effects of the communication process identified in Q2 in Distributed Software Development Projects?

The rest of the study is organized as follows: Section 2 describes the research method used in this tertiary study; Section 3 presents a detailed description of the results; Section 4 includes a discussion of the results and their implications; finally, Section 5 presents the conclusions, as well as the threats to the validation of and guidance for further studies.

2. Research Method

In this study it was used a tertiary review research method, which consists of conducting a systematic review of secondary studies and uses the same methodology of a common systematic review (Kitchenham & Charters, 2007). The tertiary systematic study was conducted in order to identify, select and analyze the most relevant and acknowledged secondary studies in the area that could answer the research questions to complement the studies identified by (Da Silva, Prikladnicki, Franca, Monteiro, Costa & Rocha, 2011).

This particular study was based on the (i) Development of the Review Protocol, (ii) Identification of Inclusion and Exclusion Criteria, (iii) Sources and Search Strategy, (iv) Selection Process for Secondary Studies, (v) Quality Evaluation, (vi) Data Extraction and (vii) Findings Summary. These stages are better detailed in the following subsections.

2.1 Review Protocol

The review protocol was developed based on the guidelines and procedures of systematic Literature Review (Kitchenham & Charters, 2007). This protocol specifies the basis for the tertiary study research questions, search strategy, selection criteria, data extraction and synthesis. The protocol was mainly developed by an author and reviewed by other authors to mitigate any source of bias.

2.2 Inclusion and Exclusion Criteria

In creating these criteria the goal is to find all relevant studies in the research. The inclusion of a work is defined by the relevance (it is believed that the work is a potential candidate to become a secondary study) in relation to the research questions, determined by title analysis, keywords, summary and conclusion. A summary of the inclusion and exclusion criteria for this tertiary study is shown in Table 1:

Table 1 - Inclusion and Exclusion Criteria

Inclusion Criteria
Studies that describe a systematic Literature Review in DSD environments;
Studies that primarily or secondarily focus on the Communication Process in distributed environments; Studies which are available for access through the online library service.
Exclusion Criteria
Irrelevant studies which do not answer the research questions.
Repeated studies: if a study is available on different search sources, the first finding will be considered; Studies with incomplete text, content and/or results.

2.3 Source and Search Strategy

Distributed Software Development has become pervasive in modern enterprises. "DSD" has generated a new era of software development by eliminating boundaries of development team thereby forming virtual teams. Thus, Distributed Software Development always generated the debate regarding the issues related to the communication, development tools, cultural differences, knowledge transfer, interation, etc. (Nisar & Hameed, 2004 in Bhalerao & Ingle, 2009).

An extensive research process was conducted in order to look for articles published between 2006 and 2010, combining the automatic search, which took place from 2006 to 2010, and the manual search from 2008 to 2010 so as to have a larger coverage. Manual search was carried out at conferences and relevant events. Researchers analyzed the title of all articles published in each source used for the manual search.

The automatic search took into account five sources: ACM Digital Library, IEEEXplore Digital Library, Elsevier ScienceDirect, El Compendex, and Scopus. All searches were automatically held by reading the title, followed by summary and conclusion and finally the full article reading. In automatic search the search terms used were built on the basis of the research questions presented in Section 1. The search terms for the research questions were developed in three stages. Firstly, keywords were identified in the questions. Secondly, synonyms for the keywords were defined by DSD consulting experts. Thirdly, the search string was built from the combination of keywords and synonyms, in which the operators OR and AND were interchangeably used. The string framing is shown in Figure 1:

Figure 1 - Search String for Secondary Studies Selection

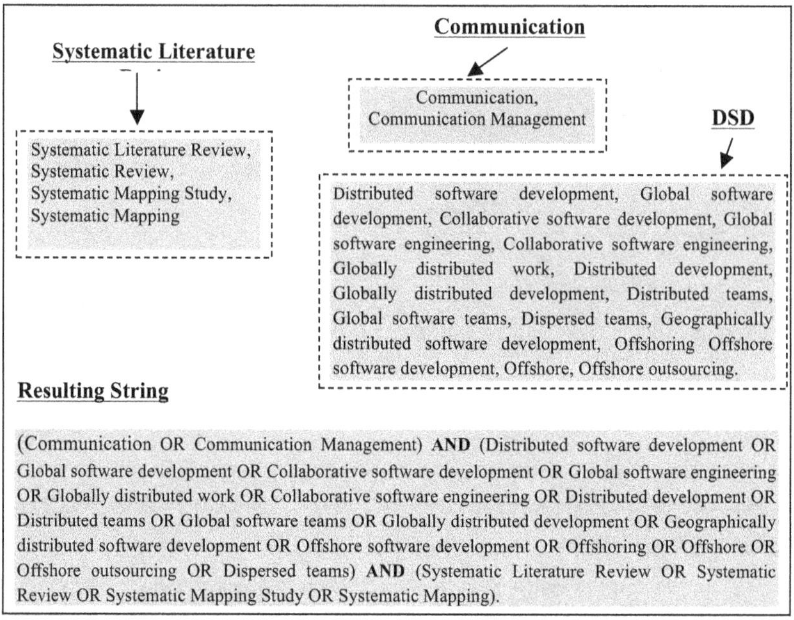

2.4 Selection Process for Secondary Studies

According to Kitchenham and Charters (2007), the initial searches show a large number of studies which are not relevant, as they do not answer to the questions, nor do they have a relation to the topic at hand. Therefore, irrelevant studies are completely put aside at first. Figure 2 shows the growth in numbers of the secondary studies selection process by searching in Da Silva, Prikladnicki, Franca, Monteiro, Costa and Rocha (2011) database, whether it is automatic or manual. Phase 1 shows the search made in database cited, in which nine secondary studies were selected in the DSD context.

Figure 2 – Selection Process For Secondary Studies

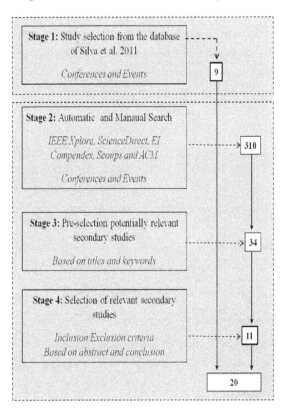

The results of the automatic and manual search are presented in Phase 2 (n = 310). These were evaluated in Phase 3 through the title and keyword analysis, as well as the exclusion of studies that were clearly not relevant to this review, resulting in 34 potentially relevant studies. In Phase 4 studies were selected based on inclusion and exclusion criteria (shown in Section 2.2), resulting in 14 articles. However, according to the analyses which were carried out, the 14 selected articles are related to 11 secondary studies, since more than one article may be related to the same secondary study. The result number of the selected studies was added to the results from Phase 1, totaling 20 studies, which were then assessed for quality.

2.5. Quality Evaluation

To lead the results interpretation referring to the included studies and determine the inferences strength, the quality reviews index was independently assessed by two researchers using an older version of the criteria set by the Centre for Reviews and Dissemination (CDR) and Database of Abstracts of Reviews of Effects (DARE), from York University (Atkins et al., 2004).

This version of the DARE criteria is based on four criteria (Table 2), which use the following levels of agreement or disagreement: 0 (not included), 0.5 (partly included) and 1 (totally included). The final quality index is calculated by the total sum of the four criteria scores, which can be visualized in Appendix C. This index is also commonly used to display the strength of evidence for extraction and data synthesis.

Table 2 - Quality Criteria

CQ1: Are the Inclusion and Exclusion criteria well described and appropriate?
CQ2: Did the literature research potentially include all the relevant studies?
CQ3: Did the included studies have their quality/validity assessed?
CQ4: Has the database/study base been adequately described?

2.6. Data Extraction

To back up data extraction and register and subsequent analysis, we used the *Mendeley* tool[9], a bibliographic reference manager. To each study a unique identifier (SE1 - SE20) was assigned. The following information was extracted from each article: publication year, authors and the country where the research was carried out.

2.7. Data Synthesis

The data synthesis process was based on the constant coding and comparison methods (Glaser & Strauss, 1967) where the studies transcriptions have a code for a

---

[9]Source: http://www.mendeley.com

given factor/effect and make up a specific category. As the data were identified, they were removed and given a unique identifier (Table 3):

Code	Mean	Description
C1...Cn	Category	A code sequentially assigned to the categories in which the factors and effects fit into the evaluated secondary studies
F1...Fn	Factor	A code sequentially assigned to the identified factors in the evaluated secondary studies.
E1...En	Effect	A code assigned to the identified effects in the evaluated secondary studies.
ES...ESn	Secondary Study	A code assigned to the evaluated secondary studies
A1...An	Articles	A code assigned to articles which are associated with a specific secondary study

Data Formatting

An encoded secondary study can be related to more than one article. This means the study was included by means of the selection process and must be encoded and associated with its respective secondary study, as shown in Appendix A. To make the synthesis of the secondary studies with more than one related article easier the following rule is adopted: the former paper is used to compile the temporal statistics and the most complete is used for data extraction.

The method of data analysis and synthesis through constant coding and comparison and Grounded Theory (GT) (Glaser & Strauss, 1967) is illustrated in Figure 3. Which exposes evidence F9: Lack of face-to-face interaction. This process began by marking key points of each secondary study transcription, being assigned a code to each key point. A code is represented by the secondary study reference, factor or corresponding effect, study page and paragraph in which the transcription was identified (E.g. 01).

Code: F9. Lack of face-to-face Interaction (ES_02, F9, 6, 3°)   (E.g. 01)

The constant comparison method is being used to group these codes and produce a higher abstraction level, through the concepts underlying GT (E.g. 02).

Concept: Face to face meeting.   (E.g 02)

Once more the constant comparison method was applied to concepts in order to produce a third abstraction level called Evidence. This level is composed of the factors and effects identified in secondary studies, which will be part of a fourth abstraction level called Category. This level is divided into three different categories: C1. (Human Factors), C2. (Infrastructure Location and Rehabilitation), C3. (Processes and Technology), where each evidence comprises a category (E.g.03).

Evidence: F9. Lack of face-to-face interaction.

Category: C1. Human Factors.   (E.g. 03)

Factor F9, i.e. Lack of face-to-face interaction, deals with presential meetings between teams within an organization. Figure 3a illustrates how the evidence F9 arose from the underlying concepts and Figure 3b shows abstraction data levels.

Figure 3 – A: Emergence of The Evidence From The Concepts / B: Levels of Abstraction

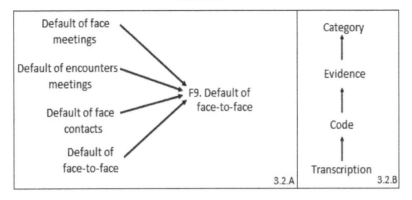

Therefore, each transcription will be identified by a code, which is related to certain evidence, and may be a factor or effect; further each evidence is associated with a given category, as shown in Figure 4, by using the example of factor F9, Lack of face-to-face interaction.

Figure 4 – Structure of The evidence according to levels of abstraction

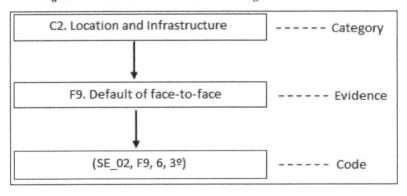

The results synthesis was organized in tables, which show the frequency of the evidence occurrence, by counting the number of times the evidence is identified in different studies.

3. The Results So Far

The next sections present an overview of the studies, the quality evaluation results, the factors and effects description and their relation identified in the communication process for DSD projects taken from a list of secondary studies.

3.1 Studies Overview

The combination of automatic and manual searches in stages 2 to 4 (Figure 2) resulted in 310 studies, from which 14 articles were selected for data extraction and analysis (Table 4). These 14 articles are related to 11 secondary studies:

Table 4 - Search Strategies, Sources and Number of Secondary Studies

Search Strategy	Source	Search Results (a)	Potentially Relevant (b)	No Access	Not Relevant	Repeated	Incomplete	Relevant Studies (c)	Search Efficacy (c/a)	First Filter Efficacy (c/b)
Automatic	IEEEXplore	83	7	0	2	0	0	5	6,0%	71%
	ScienceDirect	100	5	0	0	4	0	1	1%	20%
	EI Compendex	7	5	1	1	1	0	2	28,5%	40%
	Scopus	15	6	1	2	3	0	0	0%	0%
	ACM	5	3	2	0	1	0	0	0%	0%
Manual	Conferences and Events	100	8	0	2	0	0	6	6,0%	75%
	Total	**310**	**34**	**4**	**7**	**9**	**0**	**14**	**4,5%**	**41%**

The automatic search resulted in 57% (8/14) of the relevant studies and manual search resulted in 43% (6/14). The significant manual search number results shows that the combination of automatic and manual search strategies is essential to ensure coverage on systematic reviews and mapping studies, as can be seen in (Da Silva, Prikladnicki, Franca, Monteiro, Costa & Rocha, 2011). The overall automatic search process effectiveness is very low, since relevant studies represent only 4.5% (14/310) of the entire set of studies held in the first stage of the selection process. On the other hand, the first filter effectiveness results in a list of relevant studies, which increases significantly to 41% (14/34).

Taking into account the results of automatic and manual search, 11 secondary studies and 9 studies selected from Da Silva et al. database, this tertiary study looked at 20 secondary studies. Figure 5 shows the chronological distribution of secondary studies published between 2006 and 2010, proving that 45% (9/20) were published in 2011.

Figure 5 – Temporal Distribution of Secondary Studies

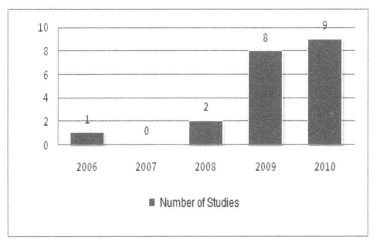

In Figure 6, secondary studies distribution was represented by 21 different institutions (academic and/or research and commercial). 20% (4/20) of representative institutions were held by Spain and Brazil. All studies were from 11 countries; where in the distribution of these institutions by country was taken into account the first author's nationality.

Figure 6 – Geographic Distribution

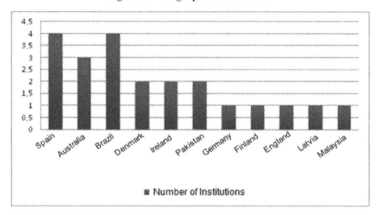

■ Number of Institutions

3.2 Secondary Studies Quality

As described in section 2.5, each study was assessed independently by two researchers according to four quality criteria. Two researchers provided scores for each criterion ranging from 0 to 4, so the quality score is obtained by summing the scores assigned to all four criteria. However, if there was a disagreement between the two researchers, a third researcher was consulted. The complete results of quality assessment are presented in Appendix C. Table 5 summarizes the quality assessment according to the four quality criteria.

Table 5 - Summary of Quality Assessment of Secundary Studies

Study Ref	Mininum Score	Maximum Score	Quartiles
SE_05, SE_11, SE_14, SE_18, SE_20	3,5	4	4th
SE_02, SE_07, SE_08, SE_10, SE_12, SE_13, SE_15, SE_19	2,5	3	3rd
SE_03, SE_04, SE_06, SE_16, SE_17	1,5	2	2nd
SE_01, SE_09	0	1	1st

Only two studies (SE_01 and SE_09) scored 1, in the first quartile, and five studies (SE_05, SE_11, SE_14, SE_18, SE_20) scored between 3.5 and 4, in the fourth quartile.

3.3 Evidence Mapping

In this section, we present the results to each research question. In Section 3.3.1 the evidence regarding the factors that influence the communication process in DSD projects are presented. In Section 3.3.2 we present the evidence on the effects identified in the communication process in DSD projects. Further, Section 3.3.3 describes the possible relationships between the factors and effects, i.e., which possible factors may cause certain effects.

All the evidences are clearly referenced by 20 secondary studies, and the reference numbers are preceded by ES[10] as a way of clarifying the systematic review references. The method used to synthesize the evidences was explained in detail in Section 2.7.

Figure 7 shows the relations between the research questions. Firstly, it presents the collected data about the factors that influence the communication process in DSD projects (Q1), and the effects of this communication (Q2) in DSD projects. Therefore, the relation between communication process factors and effects (Q3) was related to the initial evidence (Q1 and Q2).

---

[10] An acronym used in this author's original language.

Figure 7 - Relationship Between The Three Research Questions

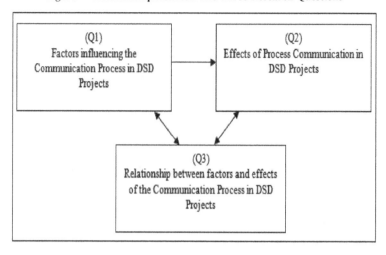

3.3.1 Q1: Which factors influence the communication process in DSD Projects?

Based on the 20 secondary studies analyzed, it was possible to identify 29 factors, which were grouped according to categories: C1. (Human Factors), C2. (Location and Infrastructure) and C3. (Processes and Technology). The graph in Figure 8 shows the distibution of these 29 factors according to the categories obtained with the extracted information from the selected secondary studies.

Figure 8 – Amount (n) Of Factors According To Their Respective Categories

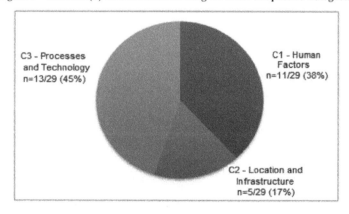

The 29 factors extracted from secondary studies are listed in Table 6, where the columns are represented by the categories created by the encoding process described in Section 2.6, factors (F1-F29) and quantity. The factors order (F1-F29) is obtained through the secondary studies amount frequency.

Table 6 - Factors in The Process of Communication Projects DDS

Categories	Factors (F1- F29)	Number of tudies %
	F1. Cultural Differences	8/20 (40%)
C1. Human	F3. Language / Linguistic Barriers	7/20 (35%)
Factors	F5. Coordination	6/20 (30%)
	F6. Visibility / Perceiving	6/20 (30%)
	F7. Informal Communication limited	6/20 (30%)
	F17. Awareness Team	2/20 (10%)
	F18. Communication skills	2/20 (10%)
	F19. Contact Networks reduced	2/20 (10%)
	F20. Definition of roles and responsibilities	2/20 (10%)
	F27. Size of Personal Networks	1/20 (5%)
	F29. Social Relations weak	1/20 (5%)
	F2. Geographic dispersion	7/20 (35%)
C2. Location	F4. Temporal distance	6/20 (30%)
and	F8. Infrastructure	5/20 (25%)
Infrastructure	F9. No face-to-face	5/20 (25%)
	F21. Synchronization of Work Schedules	1/20 (5%)
	F10. Definition of Media Communication (synchronous and asynchronous)	5/20 (25%)
	F11. Application of Agile Approaches	4/20 (20%)
	F12. Selection of Communication Technologies	4/20 (20%)
C3. Processes	F13. Distribution of tasks	4/20 (20%)
and	F14. Collaboration Tools	4/20 (20%)
Technology	F15. High-Bandwidth	2/20 (10%)
	F16. Communication Standards	2/20 (10%)
	F22. Number of Distributed Teams	1/20 (5%)
	F23. Communication Policy	1/20 (5%)

F24. Different Communication Styles	1/20 (5%)
F25. Models of Collaboration	1/20 (5%)
F26. Multiple Communication Channels	1/20 (5%)
F28. Translation Process and Coding	1/20 (5%)

Factors related to the categories "Human Factors" and "Processes and Technology" clearly dominate the results of this tertiary study. Of the 29 identified factors, 24 are related to one of these two categories. Cultural differences, geographic dispersion, language barriers and temporal distance influence directly and may intensify the problems of communication in DSD projects [SE_04] [SE_05] [SE_11] [SE_15] [SE_18]. Cultural differences can also lead to conflicting behaviors, misunderstandings, and difficulty in obtaining confidence [SE_04] [SE_05].

Geographic dispersion is directly related to the absence of face-to-face communication, since geographically distributed teams do not share the same environment, what may lead to problems such as requirements misunderstandings and lack of trust amongst team members [SE_03] [SE_04] [SE12] [SE_15].

The difference in language between the dispersed teams is seen as an additional trouble for communication and it is related to the definition of communication media (synchronous and asynchronous). There is a preference for asynchronous communication emerging from the inherent difficulty in maintaining real time communication with other teams, as they have no knowledge of the used language [SE_05] [SE_11] [SE_18].

Temporal Distance may have a great impact on running meetings between teams, causing delays in response or misunderstandings adjustment [SE_05] [SE_06] [SE_15] [SE_18], as observed in a secondary study, "working across a large number of time zones was an enormous ... this issue makes it very difficult to schedule meetings, as every time is inconvenient for someone "[SE_11]. Physical and technology infrastructure are important factors in distributed projects communication process, as the team communicates constantly. In addition, the infrastructure must be secure to ensure that intellectual property and other knowledge are not accessed by unauthorized people, as well as to guarantee a good knowledge management [SE_02] [SE_05] [SE_06] [SE_11] [SE_15].

Maintaining the teams' work visible is a difficult task, but it is necessary to make tasks and responsibilities assignment easier. The perception or awareness (knowledge about the team and its activities) depends on the awareness of the work progress,, of what is being worked on, as well as of the project progress [SE_03]] [SE_11] [SE_12] [SE_17] [SE_18].

From the discussion above, it became clear that the factors have a cause-effect relationship, and that the effects may have a direct and indirect influence on the effectiveness of the communication process in DSD. In Section 4.2, we present a conceptual model proposed to explain these cause-effect relationships and some hypotheses formulation, which can be supported by the model and evaluated in future research.

3.3.2 Q2: Which Are The Effects Identified in The Communication Process in DSD Projects?

This section presents the 25 effects identified by the survey. These were also grouped according to categories: C1. (Human Factors), C2. (Location and Infrastructure) and C3. (Processes and Technology). The graph in Figure 9 shows the division effects in accordance to their respective categories, obtained with the extracted information from the selected secondary studies.

Figure 9 - Amount (n) Of Effects According to Their Respective Categories

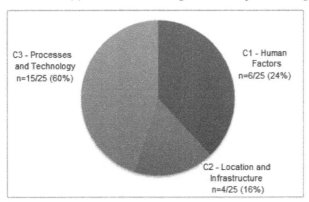

These effects, achieved with the secondary studies, were classified in two ways: negative effects are associated with non-effective communication (NEC) and positive effects are associated with Effective Communication (EC), which are listed in Table 8 in order to answer the research question Q2. The effects order (E1-E25) is obtained through the secondary studies amount frequency.

Table 7 - Effects of Process Communication Projects DDS

Categories	Classification	Effects	Number of Studies (%)
C1. Human Factors	EC. Effective Communication	E8. Personal Relationships	3/20 (15%)
		E25. Ripening Team	1/20 (5%)
	NEC. Not Effective Communication	E1. Uncertainties, misunderstandings and misconceptions	7/20 (35%)
		E3. Lack of Confidence	5/20 (25%)
		E21. Lack of team cohesion	1/20 (5%)
		E23. Low creativity	1/20 (5%)
C2. Location and Infrastructure	EC. Effective Communication	E14. Collaboration teams	2/20 (10%)
	NEC. Not Effective Communication	E16. Absence of Synchronous Communication	2/20 (10%)
		E18. High Number of Failures	2/20 (10%)
		E22. Low performance	1/20 (5%)
C3. Processes and Technology	EC. Effective Communication	E4. Quality of Communication	4/20 (20%)
		E6. Survey Process Requirements	3/20 (15%)
		E7. Sharing knowledge	3/20 (15%)
		E10. Distributed Project Management	2/20 (10%)
		E17. Project Success	2/20 (10%)
		E19. Feed-back using Scrum	2/20 (10%)
	NEC. Not Effective Communication	E2. Sharing of information limited	6/20 (30%)
		E5. Delay of Responses	4/20 (20%)
		E9. Ambiguity of Information	3/20 (15%)
		E11. Reduced Productivity	2/20 (10%)
		E12. Software Defects	2/20 (10%)

E13. Reducing Frequency of Communication	2/20 (10%)
E15. Loss of Information	2/20 (10%)
E20. Restriction of Communication	1/20 (5%)
E24. Low Quality of Decision	1/20 (5%)

Bearing in mind the effects results, it was noticeable that most of these categories are related to the "Human Factors" and "Processes and Technology". Of the 25 identified factors, 21 are related to these two categories. It is also important to note that 64% (16/25) of the effects are classified as negative, i.e., they contribute to non-effective communication (NEC).

Uncertainties and misunderstandings are caused by cultural differences which imply different terminology [SE_02] [SE_04] [SE_17]; different communication mechanisms and lack of communication standards result in misinterpretation of ideas by people involved; lack of face-to-face communication undermines the clarity of communication [SE_04] [SE_15] [SE_18]; lack of informal communication [SE_02] [SE_03] [SE_15] [SE_16] can lead to misunderstandings; and different languages [SE_03] [SE_05] [SE_18] can cause message misinterpretation.

Mutual trust is a key factor for an effective communication; in distributed environments, however, difficulty increases, due to cultural differences [SE_05] [SE_11], absence of face-to-face interaction [SE_05] [SE_18], the great number of teams [SE_01] and geographic dispersion [SE_15], since the team members hardly know each other, or their information.

Communication quality is important to clarify information, especially in distributed environments. To maintain this quality it is necessary to have an adequate infrastructure, effective tools and trusted networks for qualified information transmission [SE_05] [SE_06] [SE_13] [SE_15] [SE_18]. Furthermore, the communication quality is directly related to the project success [SE_05], as observed in a secondary study "Communication and collaborative tools are essential to the success of software development projects" [SE_18].

Some studies have highlighted the use of skillful practices in DSD context, in particular the use of Scrum, because the feedbacks are fast, contributing to knowledge and information sharing [SE_06] [SE_18].

3.3.3 Q3: What Which Factors Are Related To The Effects Identified in The Communication Process in Distributed Software Development Projects?

This question sought to relate the main factors that cause the effects identified in the communication process in DSD projects. Out of the 20 analyzed secondary studies and the 29 identified factors, 25 were associated with 23 identified effects (from the total of 25 identified by the tertiary study). The category relationship between factors and effects is mapped in Figure 10. The circles size shows how many effects are directly related to the factors corresponding to each category. For instance, there are four C1 effects (Human Factors) that relate to other C1 factors (Human Factors). The amount is indicated in the circle center.

Figure 10 - Relating Factors and Effects by Categories

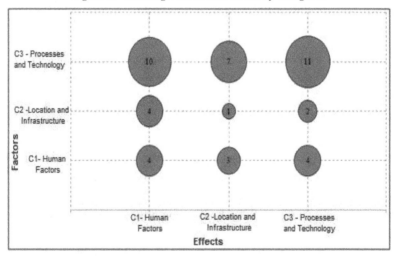

More than one effect related to the same factor was identified in the relationship between factors and effects, as well as more than one study relating the same effect to a given factor. Evidences relating to the factors and effects relationship are summarized in Table 8:

Table 8 - Communication Process Effects in DSD Projects

Factor	Effect	References – ES: Secondary Studies	Number of Studies (Reviews) (%)
F1. Cultural Differences	E1. Uncertainties, misunderstandings and misconceptions E2. Shared Information Limited E3. Lack of Confidence E16. Absence of Synchronous Communication	SE_02; SE_04; SE_05; SE_11.	4/20 (20%)
F2. Geographic Dispersion	E1. Uncertainties, misunderstandings and misconceptions E2. Shared Information Limited E3. Lack of Confidence E5. Delay of Responses E13. Communication Frequency Reduced E15. Loss of Information	SE_03; SE _04; SE _05; SE _15; SE _18; SE _19	6/20 (30%)
F3. Language/ Linguistic Barriers	E1. Uncertainties, misunderstandings and misconceptions E2. Shared Information Limited E3. Lack of Confidence E13. Communication Frequency Reduced	SE _04; SE _05; SE _18	3/20 (15%)
F4. Temporal Dispersion	E5. Delay of Responses E13. Communication Frequency Reduced E20. Restriction of Communication	SE_05; SE _06; SE_15; SE _18	4/20 (20%)
F5. Coordination	E2. Shared Information Limited	SE_02;	3/20 (15%)

	E5. Delay of Responses	SE_05;	
	E7. Shared Knowledge	SE_18	
	E14. Team Cooperation		
	E18. High Number of Failures		
	E22. Low Performance		
F6. Visibility / Perception	E2. Shared Information Limited		
	E6. Requirements Acquisition	SE_02;	
	E7. Shared Knowledge	SE_03;	
	E10. Distributed Projects Management	SE_12; SE_17;	5/20 (25%)
	E13. Communication Frequency Reduced	SE_18	
F7. Informal Communication Limited	E3. Lack of Confidence		
	E6. Requirements Acquisition	SE_02;	
	E8. Personal Relationship	SE_03;	
	E10. Distributed Projects Management	SE_05; SE_15;	5/20 (25%)
	E23. Low Creativity	SE_18	
	E24. Low Quality of Decision		
F8. Infrastructure	E2. Shared Information Limited		
	E4. Quality of Communication		
	E11. Productivity Reduced	SE_02;	
	E13. Communication Frequency Reduced	SE_05; SE_06;	4/20 (20%)
	E15. Loss of Information	SE_15	
	E20. Restriction of Communication		
F9. No *face-a-face* Interaction	E1. Uncertainties, misunderstandings and misconceptions	SE_04; SE_05;	
	E2. Shared Information Limited	SE_15;	5/20 (25%)
	E3. Lack of Confidence	SE_18;	
	E8. Personal Relationship	SE_20	

F10. Definition of Media Communication (synchronous or asynchronous)	E4. Quality of Communication E6. Requirements Acquisition E9. Ambiguity of Information E10. Distributed Projects Management	SE_03; SE_05; SE_08; SE_17; SE_18.	5/20 (25%)
F11. Application of Agile Approaches	E3. Lack of Confidence E6. Requirements Acquisition E19. Regular Feed-back regular using Scrum	SE_07; SE_18	2/20 (10%)
F12. Communication Technologies Selection	E2. Shared Information Limited E4. Quality of Communication E7. Shared Knowledge E8. Personal Relationship E10. Distributed Projects Management E14. Team Collaboration E15. Loss of Information E17. Project Success E25. Ripening Team	SE_02; SE_04; SE_05; SE_08; SE_13; SE_15; SE_19	7/20 (35%)
F13. Tasks Division	E1. Uncertainties, misunderstandings and misconceptions E7. Shared Knowledge E17. Project Success E8. Personal Relationship	SE_05; SE_18	2/20 (10%).
F14. Collaboration tools	E4. Quality of Communication E7. Shared Knowledge E8. Personal Relationship E10. Distributed Projects Management E17. Project Success E19. Regular Feed-back regular using Scrum	SE_02; SE_06; SE_18	3/20 (15%)

F15. High-Bandwidth	E4. Quality of Communication E10. Distributed Projects Management	SE_05; SE_06	2/20 (10%)
F16. Communication Patterns	E1. Uncertainties, misunderstandings and misconceptions E2. Shared Information Limited E5. Delay of Responses	SE_02; SE_05	2/20 (10%)
F17. Awareness Team	E2. Shared Information Limited E12. Software Defects	SE_02; SE_05	2/20 (10%)
F18. Communication Skills	E2. Shared Information Limited E4. Quality of Communication	SE_02; SE_18	2/20 (10%)
F19. Contact Networks	E11. Productivity Reduced E13. Communication Frequency Reduced	SE_02; SE_17	2/20 (10%)
F22. Number of Distributed teams	E3. Lack of Confidence	SE_01	1/20 (5%)
F23. Communication Policy	E19. Regular Feed-back regular using Scrum	SE_06	1/20 (5%)
F24. Different Communication Styles	E1. Uncertainties, misunderstandings and misconceptions	SE_03	1/20 (5%)
F26. Multiple Communication Channels	E4. Quality of Communication	SE_06	1/20 (5%)
F27. Size of Personal Networks	E11. Productivity Reduced E13. Communication Frequency Reduced	SE_02	1/20 (5%)
F29. Weak Social Relations	E3. Lack of Confidence	SE_05	1/20 (5%)

Figure 11 – Mapping The Relationship Between Factors and Effects by Category

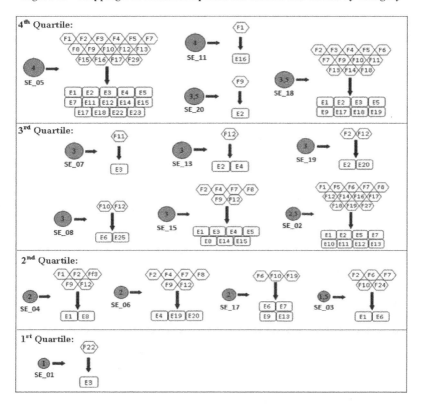

Figure 11 demonstrates, in more detail and in accordance with the quality index and the quartile, the relationship between factors and effects, highlighting the factors that are related to specific effects according to the evidence identified in their respective secondary studies. The quality index is indicated in the circle center.

4. Analysis of Results

4.1 Analogy to Carmel's Approach

This section shows an analogy to Carmel's approach (Carmel, 1999), which addresses the centrifugal forces, factors that can lead a distributed team to failure, and centripetal forces, factors that can lead the team to success. This analogy was carried out according to the factors and effects identified in the study, as can be seen in Figure 12.

Figure 12 - Analogy to Carmel Approach Using The Factors and Effects Identified in The Research.

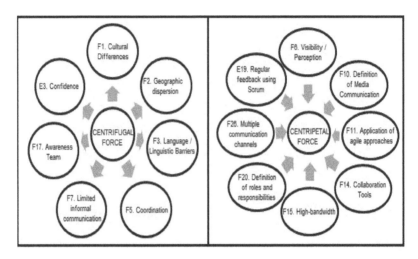

Source: Adapted From Carmel (1999) with the data collected from the tertiary study

Amongst the 29 identified factors and the 25 identified effects, some stand out: F1. Cultural Differences, F2. Geographic Dispersion, F3. Language barriers, F4. Temporal Distance, F5. Coordination, F7. Limited Informal Communication and F17. Team Awareness; and concerning the effects, there is E5. Trust as centrifugal forces, which can cause a distributed team to fail. The factors F6. Visibility/Perception, F10. Communication Media Definition (synchronous and asynchronous), F11. Skillful Approacches Application, F14. Collaboration Tools, F15. High bandwidth, F20. Roles and Responsibilities Definition and F26. Multiple Communication Channels and the effect E19. Regular feedback using Scrum, that stands out as a centripetal force, which may lead a distributed team to success.

With this analogy it was possible to conclude that, even after about 12 years, some factors, such as F1. Cultural Differences and F2. Geographic Dispersion, persist as centrifugal forces, as well as the inclusion of new factors according to the evidence shown by the secondary studies. Likewise, factor F14. Collaboration Tools persists as a centripetal force.

Given this context, one can see that, even with the whole globalization process, it is clear that the communication process is important to guide the project in distributed environments. Nevertheless, obtaining and keeping an effective communication is not an easy task.

4.2 Conceptual Model of the Communication Process Effectiveness in DSD Projects

The analysis of the evidence relating to factors in the communication process in DSD projects revealed that the factors can be interpreted as variable. Using this information, a conceptual model of the communication process effectiveness in DSD Projects was built.

To achieve this conceptual model, a chain of cause-effect relationships can be developed to convey the impact of certain factors on the overall communication process effectiveness. This model was developed to explain these cause-effect relations based on the method presented by (SJØBERG et al., 2008), after four steps, and using an approach similar to that used in (Da Silva, Prikladnicki, Franca, Monteiro, Costa & Rocha, 2011).

Step 1: Identification of the factors in the model. In particular, we took into account the factors that could be interpreted as indicators of the communication process effectiveness;

Step 2: The factors were grouped according to their effect on other factors, in accordance with the secondary studies evidence. At this stage, we identified seven categories, which will consist of certain factors;

Step 3: From the evidence provided by the secondary studies, cause-effect relationships amongst the factors categories were built;

Step 4: Some proposals or hypotheses were developed based on the evidence shown by the secondary studies and on other theoretical literature studies (model is shown in Figure 13):

Figure 13. Workgroup in DSD

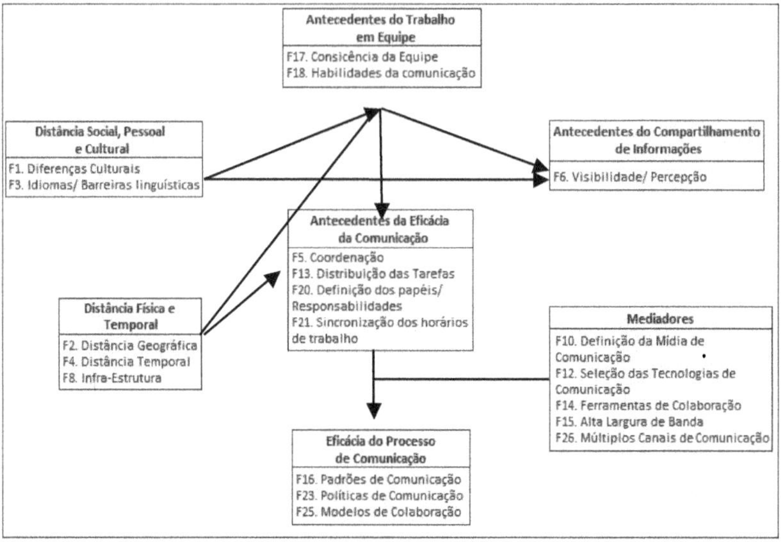

Antecedentes do Trabalho em Equipe
F17. Consiciência da Equipe
F18. Habilidades da comunicação

Distância Social, Pessoal e Cultural
F1. Diferenças Culturais
F3. Idiomas/ Barreiras linguísticas

Antecedentes do Compartilhamento de Informações
F6. Visibilidade/ Percepção

Antecedentes da Eficácia da Comunicação
F5. Coordenação
F13. Distribuição das Tarefas
F20. Definição dos papéis/ Responsabilidades
F21. Sincronização dos horários de trabalho

Distância Física e Temporal
F2. Distância Geográfica
F4. Distância Temporal
F8. Infra-Estrutura

Mediadores
F10. Definição da Mídia de Comunicação
F12. Seleção das Tecnologias de Comunicação
F14. Ferramentas de Colaboração
F15. Alta Largura de Banda
F26. Múltiplos Canais de Comunicação

Eficácia do Processo de Comunicação
F16. Padrões de Comunicação
F23. Políticas de Comunicação
F25. Modelos de Colaboração

The elements related to the social, cultural and personal distance category affect certain factors in a different way than the elements relating to physical and temporal distance. These elements are expressed by the following hypotheses:

Hypothesis 1: Temporal/ Physical Distance and also Social, Cultural and Personal Distance have a direct effect on the Teamwork Background.

Hypothesis 2: Social, Cultural and Personal Distance have a direct effect on the Information Sharing Background.

Hypothesis 3: Temporal/ Physical Distance has only an indirect effect on the Information Sharing Background through its effect on the Teamwork Background.

In this proposed model, it became necessary to divide the factors related to the communication process in DSD projects into two groups, as the evidence shows that a group of factors influence the factors of the other group. This is expressed by the following hypothesis:

Hypothesis 4: The effect related to the category of Communication Effectiveness in the Communication Process Effectiveness Background is mediated by the communication media, different technologies, collaboration tools, high bandwidth and multiple communication channels.

This model of the communication process in DSD projects effectiveness is a conceptual proposal which has not been tested by empirical studies yet. However, the compilation of evidences identified in secondary studies provides some confidence level to its legitimacy. Moreover, the stated proposals are only examples of possible relationships between the categories. Consequently not all the cause-effect relationships have generated hypotheses. Therefore, further research is needed to refine and test these hypotheses and others that may derive from this model.

5. Proposal of Good Practices

A literature research was carried out concerning various authors of the area, to set the good practices to mitigate failures in DSD projects. These set of practices are listed below:

- Start the project with a meeting face so that all members of teams know each other. Furthermore, the project manager should define properly the role and responsibilities of each within the project;
- Meeting face to face whenever possible. As a suggestion meetings may happen about every 3 or 4 months;
- Frequent synchronous meetings through tools providing teleconferencing, videoconferencing, among others. In such a way, it reduce "the distance" between the project teams, avoiding, further, the discouragement;
- Keep a default common language to all. Provide an English businesses course for training and development of language in the team. Try to unify teams with similar cultures to work together when necessary;
- Plan carefully and choose the tools that will be used in communication in distributed projects to minimize possible interference;

- Create a knowledge base (such as web portals) to gather information from a common source and allow teams to access the monitoring project in a centralized way, besides having all the members information in the database. It is worth to institutionalize the outcome for all participants of the project. Also, open a channel to informal comments among teams, leaders and project manager;
- Standardization of development processes for distributed teams;
- Appointment of technical leaders of each team. In this way, it is created an interlocutor to be the channel of communication with the DSD project management.

6. Final Considerations

This review examined 310 studies, of which 20 answered to the survey questions and were considered of acceptable quality and relevance. Of the 20 studies, 29 factors and 25 effects were identified and it was concluded that they are related to the communication process in DSD projects. Additionally, out of the 29 identified factors, 25 were associated with 23 of the 25 effects identified in the tertiary study.

The results of this study contribute to a tertiary vision and to a more comprehensive understanding of the factors and effects of the communication process in DSD projects. Nevertheless, these results also show that there are some gaps in this field what may be understood as a good chance for further research. Moreover, taking into account the identified evidences which are based on this tertiary study protocol, this research can help practitioners and researchers to identify relevant factors and effects to the communication process in DSD projects.

The approach to the communication process in DSD projects still requires more research, especially to support professionals and researchers in identifying the factors that influence the communication process and in minimizing the possible effects of the communication process identified by secondary studies in experimental and industrial environments.

7. Tertiary Study Limitations

The most common systematic reviews and mapping limitations are the possible bias introduced in the selection process and data extraction inaccuracies. These are also the possible main limitations of this study. The developed research protocol is the measure taken to avoid the studies selection bias. The combination between automatic search on multiple search sources and manual search improves the exposure of the selection process, reducing a possible bias. Research and selection process at all stages were dealt with by at least two researchers, and the conflicts in the selection process have been solved either by a third party or by consensus meetings.

The data extraction is also considered a challenge due to the great diversity in form, style and content of the analyzed secondary studies. There was little structure and content standardization, what led to the possible inaccuracy in the data extracted from secondary studies. In several studies, important data were not explicitly presented, forcing the information reading, thus making possible the inaccuracy in the data extracted from the secondary studies. Another contributions of this work was good practices selection to the support researchers and professionals in the DSD context about communication.

7.1 Future Studies

The relevance of a study can also be evaluated in terms of the future gains it may provide. Therefore, bearing in mind such importance and this study results, we provide some guidance to further research:

- It is common in qualitative analysis to check members' performance (member checking), in order to verify the extraction accuracy and the evidence synthesis. Through a project like this we could interview (using online tools) the secondary studies authors so as to gather their assessment about the synthesis obtained from their studies;

- To associate the factors which influence the communication process to possible practices in order to reduce the identified effects and, consequently, to improve communication in DSD projects;

- To test the conceptual model with empirical studies so as to refine these assumptions and others that may derive from the model;

- Finally, specific studies relating to some of the factors often cited by the evidences may be developed, with a focus mainly directed to one or more effects. At the same time the relationship between factors and effects may be more deepened.

8. Acknowledgments

UNIVERSIDADE FEDERAL RURAL DE PERNAMBUCO

References

Anandarajan, M. & Anandarajan, A. (2010). e-Research collaboration: Theory, techniques and challenges. New York: Springer.

Atkins, D., Eccles, M., Flottorp, S., Guyatt, GH., Henry, D. et al. (2004). Systems For Grading The Quality of Evidence and The Strength of Recommendations I: Critical Appraisal of Existing Approaches. The Grade Working Group. BMC Health Serv Res. 2004, pp. 4-38

Audy, J. & Prikladnicki, R. (2007). Desenvolvimento Distribuído de Software: Desenvolvimento de Software com Equipes Distribuídas. Rio de Janeiro: Elsevier.

Barbosa, S. & Canesso, N. (2004). Política e participação nas cidades digitaise comunidades em rede. In Lemos, A. (Org.) (2004). Cibercidades – As cidades na cibercultura, pp.175-206. Rio de Janeiro: E-papers.

Betz, S. & Makio, J. (2007). Amplification of the COCOMO II regarding Offshore Software Projects. In Proceedings of the Workshop on Offshoring of Software Development – Methods and Tools for Risk Management – at Second International Conference on Global Software Engineering, Munich, August 2007.

Bhalerao, S. & Ingle, M. (2009). Agile Communication Model for Distributed Software Development. Journal of Computer Science Engineering and Information Technology, vol. 1 (3), ITM University.

Binder, J. C. (2007). Global Project Management: Communication, Collaboration and Management Across Borders. Gower Publishing.

Carmel, E. (1999). Global Software Teams – Collaborating Across Borders and Time-Zones. US: Prentice Hall.

Carmel, E. & Tjia, P. (2005). Offshoring Information Technology: Sourcing and Outsourcing to a Global Workforce. New York: Cambridge University Press.

Chiavenato, I. (2004). Teoria Geral da Administração. Rio de Janeiro: Elservier.

Da Silva, F. Q. B., Costa, C., França, A. C. C. & Prikladnicki, R. (2010). Challenges and Solutions in Distributed Software Development Project Management: A Systematic Literature Review, IEEE Int. Conference on Global Software Engineering, pp. 87-96, August 2010.

Da Silva, F. Q. B., Prikladnicki, R., Franca, P. C. P., Monteiro, C. V. F., Costa, C. & Rocha, R. (2011). Research and Practice of Distributed Software Development Project Management: A Systematic Literature Review. Submitted to The Journal of Software Maintenance and Evolution, 2011.

Farias Júnior, I. H. (2008). Uma Proposta de Boas Práticas do Processo de Comunicação para Projetos de Desenvolvimento Distribuído. Master Dissertation. Recife: Universidade Federal de Pernambuco.

Glaser, B. G. & Strauss, A.L. (1967). The Discovery of Grounded Theory: Strategies for Qualitative Research. Chicago: Aldine Publishing.

Gosciola, V. (2003). Roteiro Para as Novas Mídias – Do Game à Televisão Interativa. São Paulo: Senac São Paulo.

Haesbaert, R. (2004). O Mito da Desterritorialização: Do — Fim dos Territórios à Multiterritorialidade. Rio de Janeiro: Bertrand Brasil.

Herbsleb, J. D. & Moita, D. (2001). Global Software Development. IEEE Software Magazine, IEEE Computer Society, EUA, March/April 2001.

Herbsleb, J. D. (2007). Global Software Engineering: The Future of Socio-Technical Coordination, 29th Int. Conference on Software Engineering, pp. 188-198, 2007.

Hoda, R., Nobel, J. & Marshall, S. (2011). The Impact of Inadequate Customer Collaboration on Self-Organizing Agile Teams. Journal Information and Software Technology, vol. 53, Issue 5, pp. 521-534, May 2011.

Howe, J. (2009). O Poder das Multidões – Por Que a Força da Coletividade Está Remodelando o Futuro dos Negócios. Rio de Janeiro: Elsevier.

Institute imedea networks (Image of Cover Book). Retrieved on May 24, 2013, from «http://www.networks.imdea.org/whats-new/news/2013/prophet-project-increasing-network-reliability-our-interconnected-society».

Kitchenham, B. & Charters, S. (2007), Guidelines for performing Systematic Literature Reviews in Software Engineering, Technical Report EBSE 2007-1, Keele University and Durham University Joint Report.

Komi-sirviö, S. & Tihinen, M. (2005). Lessons Learned by Participants of Distributed Software Development. Journal Knowledge and Process Management, vol. 12 n° 2 pp. 108–122, 2005.

Lévy, P. (2010). Cibercultura. São Paulo: Editora 34.

Laclau, E. & Luhmann, N. (2006). Pós-Fundacionismo – Abordagem Sistêmica e as Organizações Sociais. Porto Alegre: EDIPUCRS.

Lemos, A. & Cunha, P. (Orgs). (2003). Cibercultura. Alguns pontos para compreender a nossa época. In Lemos, A. & Cunha, P. (2003). Olhares sobre a Cibercultura, pp. 11-23. Porto Alegre: Sulina.

Mulcahy, R. (2005). PMP Exam Prep for the PMBOK Guide. Third Edition. US: RMC Publications.

Oliveira, M. (2011). Como fazer – Projetos, Relatórios, Monografias, Dissertações, Teses. Rio de Janeiro: Elsevier.

Pichler, H. (2007). Be Successful, Take a Hostage or Outsourcing The Outsourcing Manager. Proc. Second IEEE International Conference on Global Software Engineering, ICGSE, pp. 156-161, 2007.

Prikladnicki, R. (2003). MuNDDoS - Um Modelo de Referência para Desenvolvimento Distribuído de Software. Master Dissertation. Porto Alegre: PUC Rio Grande do Sul.

Prikladnicki, R., Damian, D., & Audy, J. L. N. (2008). Patterns of Evolution in the Practice of Distributed Software Development: Quantitative Results from a Systematic Review. EASE'08 Proceedings of the 12th international conference on Evaluation and Assessment in Software Engineering, London, pp.100-109, 2008.

PMI. (2008). A Guide to the Project Management Body of Knowledge. US: Project Management Institute, Inc.

Revista Superinteressante (2005). Simulacros e simulação. Retrieved on December 12, 2013, from «http://super.abril.com.br/cultura/simulacros-simulacao-446017.shtml».

Sailwal, B. (2009). Importance of Knowledge Management in Distributed Software Development. Växjö University: School of Mathematics and Systems Engineering (Reports from MSI- Rapporter från MSI).

Silva, R., Santana, A. & Patrícia, R. (2007). Um Retrato da Gestão de Pessoas em Projetos de Software: Uma Visão do Gerente vs. Desenvolvedor. XXI Simpósio Brasileiro de Engenharia de Software, João Pessoa, 2007.

Sjøberg D.I.K., Dybå T., Anda, B.C.D. & Hannay J. (2008). Building Theories in Software Engineering, pp. 312-336. In Shull F. et al. (Ed). Guide to advanced empirical software engineering, Chapter 12. Springer-Verlag, London, 2008.

Torres, A. (2011). Por um Conhecimento Livre: O Papel das Tecnologias Digitais na Defesa da Democratização das Informações. Retrieved on November 1, 2013, from «http://www.snh2011.anpuh.org/resources/anais/14/1300211280_ARQUIVO_ArtigoA NPUHAraceleTorres.pdf».

Trindade, C. C. M., Meira, A. K. O. & Lemos, S. (2008). Comunicação em Equipes Distribuídas de Desenvolvimento de Software: Revisão Sistemática. 5th Experimental Software Engineering Latin American Workshop (ESELAW), 2008.

Teixeira, M. (2013). Cyberculture: From Plato The The Virtual Universe. The Architecture of Collective Intelligence. Munich: Grin Verlag.

Teixeira, M. (2012). As faces da comunicação. Munich: Grin Verlag.

Vanassi, G. (2007). Podcasting Como Processo Midiático Interativo. Biblioteca Online de Ciências da Comunicação. Retrieved on November 17, 2013, from «www.bocc.ubi.pt/pag/vanassi-gustavo-podcasting-processo-midiatico-interativo.pdf».

Virilio, P. (1993). O espaço crítico. São Paulo: Editora 34.

Wiener, N. (1984). Cibernética e Sociedade – O Uso Humano de Seres Humanos. São Paulo: Cultrix.

APPENDIX A – Secondary Studies

ID	REF	YEAR	Reference
ES_01	[A1]	2008	SMITE, D.; WOHLIN, C.; FELDT, R.; GORSCHEK, T. "Reporting Empirical Research in Global Software Engineering: A Classification Scheme," Global Software Engineering, 2008. ICGSE 2008. IEEE International Conference, vol., no., pp.173-181, 17-20 Aug. 2008. doi: 10.1109/ICGSE.2008.22.
ES_02	[A2]	2009	JIMÉNEZ, M.; PIATTINI, M.; VIZCAÍNO, A. "Challenges and Improvements in Distributed Software Development: A Systematic Review," Advances in Software Engineering, vol. 2009, Article ID 710971, 14 pages, 2009. doi:10.1155/2009/710971.
ES_03	[A3]	2009	EBLING, T.; AUDY, J. L. N.; PRIKLADNICKI, R. "A Systematic Literature Review of Requirements Engineering in Distributed Software Development Environments". ICEIS 2009 - Proceedings of the 11th International Conference on Enterprise Information Systems, Volume ISAS, Milan, Italy, May 6-10, 2009: 363-366
ES_04	[A4]	2009	KHAN, S.U.; NIAZI, M.; AHMAD, R. "Critical Barriers for Offshore Software Development Outsourcing Vendors: A Systematic Literature Review," Software Engineering Conference, 2009. APSEC '09. Asia- Pacific, vol., no., pp.79-86, 1-3 Dec. 2009 doi: 10.1109/APSEC.2009.16
	[A5]	2009	KHAN, S. U.; NIAZI, M.; AHMAD, R. "Critical Success Factors for Offshore Software Development Outsourcing Vendors: A Systematic Literature Review." In Proceedings of the 2009 Fourth IEEE International Conference on Global Software Engineering (ICGSE '09). IEEE Computer Society, Washington, DC, USA, 207-216. DOI=10.1109/ICGSE.2009.28

ES_05	[A6]	2009	PERSSON, J.S.; MATHIASSEN, L.; BOEG, J.; MADSEN, T.S.; STEINSON, F. "Managing Risks in Distributed Software Projects: An Integrative Framework," Engineering Management, IEEE Transactions on, vol.56, no.3, pp.508-532, Aug. 2009. doi: 10.1109/TEM.2009.2013827
ES_06	[A7]	2009	HOSSAIN, E.; BABAR, M. A.; PAIK, H. "Using Scrum in Global Software Development: A Systematic Literature Review." In Proceedings of the 2009 Fourth IEEE International Conference on Global Software Engineering (ICGSE '09). IEEE Computer Society, Washington, DC, USA, 175-184 DOI=10.1109/ICGSE.2009.25 Retrieved on December 14, 2013, from http://dx.doi.org/10.1109/ICGSE.2009.25
	[A8]		HOSSAIN, E.; BABAR, M. A.; PAIK, H.; VERNER, J. "Risk Identification and Mitigation Processes for Using Scrum in Global Software Development: A Conceptual Framework," APSEC, pp.457-464, 2009 16th Asia-Pacific Software Engineering Conference, 2009. http://doi.ieeecomputersociety.org/10.1109/APSEC.2009.56
ES_07	[A9]	2010	SMITE, D.; WOHLIN, C.; GORSCHEK, T.; FELDT, R. "Empirical evidence in global software engineering: a systematic review." Empirical Software Engineering. 15, 1 (February 2010), 91-118. DOI=10.1007/s10664-009- 9123-y.
ES_08	[A10]	2010	PRIKLADNICKI, R.; AUDY, J. L. N. Process models in the practice of distributed software development: A Systematic review of the literature. Information and Software Technology 52 (2010) 779–791. doi:10.1016/j.infsof.2010.03.009.
ES_09	[A11]	2006	YALAHO, A. "A Conceptual Model of ICT-Supported Unified Process of International Outsourcing of Software Production," Enterprise Distributed Object Computing Conference Workshops, IEEE International, p. 47, 10th

			IEEE International Enterprise Distributed Object Computing Conference Workshops (EDOCW'06), 2006.
ES_10	[A12]	2009	COSTA, C.; CUNHA, C.; ROCHA, R.; FRANÇA, A.; FABIO Q. B da SILVA; PRIKLADNICK, R. "Models and Tools for Managing Distributed Software Development: A Systematic Literature Review". 14th International Conference on Evaluation and Assessment in Software Engineering (EASE 2010), April 2010.
ES_11	[A13]	2010	COSTA, C.; ROCHA, R.; FABIO Q. B da SILVA; PRIKLADNICK, R. Desafios e Boas Práticas para o Gerenciamento de Projetos no Desenvolvimento Distribuído de Software. IV Workshop de Desenvolvimento Distribuido de Software – WDDS. Setembro de 2010.
	[A14]	2010	da Silva, Fabio Q. B.; Costa, Catarina; França, A. César C.; Prikladnicki, Rafael. "Challenges and Solutions in Distributed Software Development Project Management: a Systematic Literature Review". In Proceedings of the Fifth IEEE International Conference on Global Software Engineering (ICGSE '10). IEEE Computer Society, Washington, DC, USA, 87-96. doi: 10.1109/ICGSE.2010.18
ES_12	[A15]	2009	LOPEZ, A.; NICOLAS, J.; TOVAL, A. Risks and Safeguards for the Requirements Engineering Process in Global Software Development. In Proceeding of the 2009 Fourth IEEE International Conference on Global Software Engineering (ICGSE '09). IEEE Computer Society Washington, DC, USA, 394-399 doi:10.1109/ICGSE.2009.62
ES_13	[A16]	2010	FAUZI, S.; BANNERMAN, P.; STAPLES, M. "Software Configuration Management in Global Software Development: A Systematic Map," APSEC, 404-413, 2010 Asia Pacific Software Engineering Conference, 2010.

			Retrieved on December 12, 2013, from http://doi.ieeecomputersociety.org/10.1109/APSEC.2010.53
ES_14	[A17]	2010	MONASOR, M.; VIZCAÍNO, A.; PIATTINI, M.; CABALLERO, I. "Preparing Students and Engineers for Global Software Development: A Systematic Review". Global Software Engineering, 2008. ICGSE 2008. IEEE International Conference, vol., no., pp.177-186, 23-26 Aug. 2010. doi: 10.1109/ICGSE.2010.28.
ES_15	[A18]	2010	NOLL, J.; BEECHAM, S.; RICHARDSON, I. "Global software development and collaboration: barriers and solutions" In: Proceeding of the Magazine ACM Inroads, ACM New York, NY, USA, 66 – 78, Sep. 2010. doi: 10.1145/1835428.1835445.
ES_16	[A19]	2010	ALI, N.; BEECHAM, S.; MISTRÍK, I. "Architectural Knowledge Management in Global Software Development: A Review,. In Proceeding of the 2010 5th IEEE International Conference on Global Software Engineering (ICGSE 2010), 347-352. Retrieved on May 1, 2013, from http://doi.ieeecomputersociety.org/10.1109/ICGSE.2010.48
ES_17	[A20]	2008	TRINDADE, C. C. M., MEIRA, A. K. O., LEMOS, S. Comunicação em Equipes Distribuídas de Desenvolvimento de Software: Revisão Sistemática, 5th Experimental Software Engineering Latin American Workshop (ESELAW), 2008.
ES_18	[A21]	2010	JABANGWE, R.; NURDIANI, J. "Global Software Development Challenges and Mitigation Strategies: A Systematic Review and Survey Results". Master program Software engineering 120 p/Master´s program in Software engineering 120 p, 2010.
ES_19	[A22]	2010	JALALI, S.; WOHLIN, C. "Agile Practices in Global Software Engineering - A Systematic Map," 5th IEEE International Conference on Global Software Engineering (ICGSE 2010), pp.45-54.

ES_20	[A23]	2010	Alinne C. Corrêa dos Santos, Camila Cunha Borges, Fabio Q. B. da Silva, David E. S. Carneiro. Dificuldades, Fatores e Ferramentas no Gerenciamento da Comunicação em projetos de Desenvolvimento Distribuído de Software: uma Revisão Sistemática da Literatura. IV Workshop de Desenvolvimento Distribuído de Software (WDDS). Salvador, BA, 2010.
	[A24]	2010	Alinne C. Corrêa dos Santos, Camila Cunha Borges, Fabio Q. B. da Silva, David E. S. Carneiro. Estudo baseado em Evidências sobre Dificuldades, Fatores e Ferramentas no Gerenciamento da Comunicação em Projetos de Desenvolvimento Distribuído de Software. 7th Experimental Software Engineering Latin American Workshop (ESELAW), Goiania, GO, 2010.

APPENDIX B – Data Extraction Form

Study Description

1.	Study identifier	Unique id for the study
2.	Date of data extraction	
3.	Bibliographic reference	Author(s), year, title, source
4.	Country	Country of origin of research team
5.	Type of article	Journal article, Conference paper
6.	Focus of the study	People, project, organization

Study Findings

1.	Factors	Answers to Q1
2.	Effects	Answers to Q2
3.	Relationship between factors and effects	Answers to Q3

APPENDIX C – Quality Assessment Form

Critérios de Qualidade	0	0,5	1
CQ1: Os critérios de inclusão e exclusão das revisões são descritos e adequados?	□	□	□
CQ2: A pesquisa da literatura provavelmente contemplou todos os estudos relevantes?	□	□	□
CQ3: Foi realizada a avalição da qualidade/validade dos estudos incluídos?	□	□	□
CQ4: A base de dados/estudos foram descritos adequadamente?	□	□	□

APPENDIX D – Quality Assessment

Referência dos Estudos Secundários	ID	1 Critérios de Inclusão e Exclusão	2 Contemplação de todos os estudos relevantes	3 Avaliação da Qualidade/ Validade dos Estudos	4 Descrição adequada da base de dados/estudos	TOTAL	Quartil
ES_05	[A6]	1	1	1	1	4	
ES_11	[A14]	1	1	1	1	4	
ES_14	[A17]	1	0,5	1	1	3,5	4th
ES_18	[A21]	1	1	1	0,5	3,5	
ES_20	[A24]	0,5	1	1	1	3,5	
ES_07	[A9]	1	1	0	1	3	
ES_08	[A10]	1	1	0	1	3	
ES_10	[A12]	1	1	0	1	3	
ES_13	[A16]	1	1	0	1	3	3rd
ES_15	[A18]	1	0,5	1	0,5	3	
ES_19	[A22]	1	1	0	1	3	
ES_02	[A2]	0,5	1	0	1	2,5	
ES_12	[A15]	1	0,5	0	1	2,5	
ES_04	[A4]	0,5	0,5	0,5	0,5	2	
ES_06	[A7]	1	0,5	0	0,5	2	
ES_16	[A19]	1	0,5	0	0,5	2	2nd
ES_17	[A20]	1	0,5	0	1	2	
ES_03	[A3]	0,5	0,5	0	0,5	1,5	
ES_01	[A1]	0	0,5	0	0,5	1	1st
ES_09	[A11]	0	0,5	0	0,5	1